EYEWITNESS TO HISTORY

ANNE FRANK

in her own words

Gareth Stevens
Publishing

By Caroline Kennon

Please visit our website, www.garethstevens.com. For a free color catalog of all our high-quality books, call toll free 1-800-542-2595 or fax 1-877-542-2596.

Library of Congress Cataloging-in-Publication Data

Kennon, Caroline.
Anne Frank in her own words / by Caroline Kennon.
   p. cm. — (Eyewitness to history)
Includes index.
ISBN 978-1-4824-3276-3 (pbk.)
ISBN 978-1-4824-3277-0 (6-pack)
ISBN 978-1-4339-9872-0 (library binding)
1. Frank, Anne, — 1929-1945 — Juvenile literature. 2. Holocaust, Jewish (1939-1945) — Netherlands — Amsterdam — Biography — Juvenile literature. 3. Jews — Netherlands — Amsterdam — Biography — Juvenile literature. I. Title.
DS135.N6 K46 2014
940.53—dc23

First Edition

Published in 2014 by
Gareth Stevens Publishing
111 East 14th Street, Suite 349
New York, NY 10003

Designer: Katelyn E. Reynolds
Editor: Therese Shea

Photo credits: Cover, pp. 1 (Anne) Otto Frank/Life Magazine/Time & Life Pictures/Getty Images; cover, p. 1 (background illustration) Galerie Bilderwelt/Getty Images; cover, p. 1 (logo quill icon) Seamartini Graphics Media/Shutterstock.com; cover, p. 1 (logo stamp) YasnaTen/Shutterstock.com; cover, p. 1 (color grunge frame) DmitryPrudnichenko/Shutterstock.com; cover, pp. 1-32 (paper background) Nella/Shutterstock.com; cover, pp. 1-32 (decorative elements) Ozerina Anna/Shutterstock.com; pp. 1-32 (wood texture) Reinhold Leitner/Shutterstock.com; pp. 1-32 (open book background) Elena Schweitzer/Shutterstock.com; pp. 1-32 (bookmark) Robert Adrian Hillman/Shutterstock.com; p. 5 (both) iStockphoto/Thinkstock.com; p. 7 Fred Ramage/Keystone Features/Getty Images; p. 9 (star patch) Naci Yavuz/Shutterstock.com; pp. 8-9 (photo) OFF/AFP/Getty Images; p. 10 (signature) Scewing/Wikipedia.com; pp. 10-11, 29 Andreas Rentz/Getty Images; p. 13 mifaimoltosorridere/E+/Getty Images; pp. 15, 17 Anne Frank Fonds/Anne Frank House via Getty Images; pp. 18-19 Sergio Pitamitz/age fotostock/Getty Images; p. 21 Anne Frank Fonds-Basel/Anne Frank House-Amsterdam/Getty Images; pp. 22-23 dinosmichail/Shutterstock.com; pp. 24-25 Keystone-France/Gamma-Keystone via Getty Images; p. 27 Nigel Treblin/AFP/Getty Images.

Printed in the United States of America

CPSIA compliance information: Batch #CW14GS: For further information contact Gareth Stevens, New York, New York at 1-800-542-2595.

CONTENTS

*Words in the glossary appear in **bold** type the first time they are used in the text.*

ANNE FRANK'S
Early Life

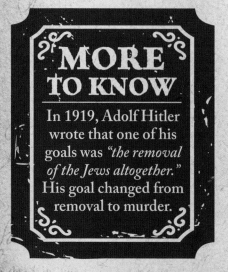
Anne Frank was born in Frankfurt, Germany, on June 12, 1929. Her parents were Edith and Otto, and she had an older sister named Margot. However, when Adolf Hitler became German **chancellor** in 1933 and then president in 1934, the Franks' lives changed forever. The Franks were Jewish, and Hitler and the **Nazi** party wrongly blamed Jews for events such as World War I as well as Germany's struggling economy.

Anne kept a diary beginning in 1942. On June 20 of that year, she wrote: *"Writing in a diary is a really strange experience for someone like me. Not only because I've never written anything before, but also because it seems to me that later on neither I nor anyone else will be interested in the musings of a thirteen-year-old schoolgirl."* Anne's diary would become world famous.

ANNE FRANK · 12.6.1929 · 31.3.1945
1979

Anne Frank can be found on postage stamps in Europe.

GERMAN AND JEWISH

Anne wrote passionately about her background. She was very aware of the hatred toward the Jews. It upset her that her fellow countrymen could hate her. On October 9, 1942, she wrote: *"Fine specimens of humanity, those Germans, and to think I'm actually one of them! No, that's not true, Hitler took away our nationality long ago. And besides, there are no greater enemies on earth than the Germans and Jews."*

ANNE FRANK

nederland

60 c

In 1933, Otto Frank moved to the Netherlands, where he set up a new business. The rest of the family soon followed. Otto believed they would be safer from the Nazis in the city of Amsterdam. Anne immediately began school in the city and resumed a normal life. Even though they felt homesick, the Franks had happy years in Amsterdam. Margot and Anne had friends of all different religions.

MORE TO KNOW

The Franks were among 300,000 Jewish people who left Germany between 1933 and 1939.

A BOOKWORM AND A PRANKSTER

Anne was outspoken and had a lot of energy. In school, she showed a love for reading and writing. However, her school friend Hannah "Hanneli" Goslar said that Anne didn't like showing other people what she wrote. Anne was also always ready to have fun. She played hopscotch, tag, and Ping-Pong. One of her favorite pranks was to throw water from her apartment building window onto people on the street below.

However, all was not peaceful. Anne wrote in her diary that many of their *"relatives in Germany were suffering under Hitler's anti-Jewish laws."* In November 1938, the Nazis burned **synagogues** as well as Jewish homes and businesses in Germany. The event became known as *Kristallnacht*, or "Night of Broken Glass."

6

These are the ruins of a synagogue in Berlin. It was burned during Kristallnacht and later hit by bombs.

7

INVASION

In 1939, World War II began with the German invasion of Poland. The Nazis then invaded Norway, Denmark, and the Netherlands. After 5 days of fighting, the Netherlands surrendered. Anne was 10 years old.

Anne and her family were in great danger. She wrote in her diary: *After May 1940 the good times were few and far between. . . . Our freedom was severely restricted by a series of anti-Jewish decrees. . . . You couldn't do this and you couldn't do that, but life went on.*

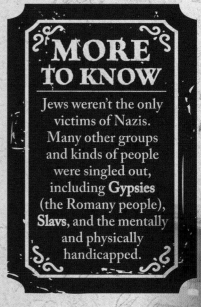

MORE TO KNOW

Jews weren't the only victims of Nazis. Many other groups and kinds of people were singled out, including **Gypsies** (the Romany people), **Slavs**, and the mentally and physically handicapped.

The Nazis destroyed property and put up signs on businesses that said: "No Jews Allowed." Jewish children had to go to Jewish schools. At her new school, Anne made many friends. She played Monopoly, read books, and visited the Jewish ice-cream parlor.

Jewish people had to sew badges like this on their clothing during World War II.

ANTI-JEWISH DECREES

The Nazis made rules that Jews in Amsterdam were required to follow. Anne wrote them down: Jews had to wear a yellow star. They were forbidden to use streetcars. They were only allowed to do their shopping between the hours of 3 p.m. and 5 p.m. They weren't allowed to walk in the parks, use public swimming pools, or go to movies or plays. They even had to turn in their bicycles.

a Jewish business in Berlin in 1930

ANNE AND
Her Diary

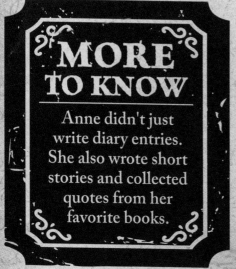

MORE TO KNOW

Anne didn't just write diary entries. She also wrote short stories and collected quotes from her favorite books.

On Anne's thirteenth birthday, her parents gave her a small red-and-white checkered diary that she became attached to. Anne wrote in it often, calling it "Kitty" and pretending it was a friend. She wanted it to be someone she could turn to. She talked to the diary: *"I'll begin from the moment I got you, the moment I saw you lying on the table among my other birthday presents."*

Anne loved her birthday present and thought of it as a friend.

Anne's actual signature:

Anne Frank

As the tensions of the war grew and the difficulties for the Jews became worse, Anne's diary became even more important to her. Their home in Amsterdam was becoming less safe every day. As Anne wrote to Kitty in her diary about their troubles, her father soon realized that their family was once again in danger.

SWEET 13

Otto and Edith Frank tried to make Anne's thirteenth birthday very special in order to make up for the scary world their daughter was living in. They threw a birthday party for her and her friends. Since Jews couldn't go to the movie theater anymore, they invited Anne's friends over to watch a movie. They wanted to make sure that Anne and Margot led as normal of a life as possible during the war.

The SECRET ANNEX

Otto Frank had a plan. Anne wrote on July 5, 1942: *"A few days ago, as we were taking a stroll around our neighborhood square, Father began to talk about going into hiding. He said it would be very hard for us to live cut off from the rest of the world."*

Anne had many questions: *"Hiding . . . where would we hide? In the city? In the country? In a house? In a shack? When, where, how . . .? These were questions I wasn't allowed to ask, but they still kept running through my mind."*

With the help of a few of Otto's employees, the Franks moved into an attic apartment Anne called the "secret **annex**" on July 6, 1942. Anne and her family spent the next 2 years there.

MOVING TO THE ANNEX

The Franks left their apartment very early in the morning wearing multiple layers of clothes. Anne said it *"looked as if we were going off to spend the night in a refrigerator."* She explained that this was a clever way of taking as many clothes to the annex as they could: *"No Jew in our situation would dare leave the house with a suitcase full of clothes."* The authorities would immediately know they were trying to flee.

MORE TO KNOW

A lot of Jewish families went into hiding like the Franks did. Jews that were caught hiding were severely punished. Any non-Jews helping Jews hide could also be arrested.

A statue of Anne Frank was later raised in front of the building where the Frank family hid.

THE VAN PELS
Family

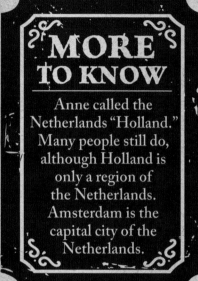

MORE TO KNOW

Anne called the Netherlands "Holland." Many people still do, although Holland is only a region of the Netherlands. Amsterdam is the capital city of the Netherlands.

Soon the van Pels family moved into the annex, too. Hermann van Pels was Otto's business partner and friend. He brought his wife, Auguste, and their son, Peter. Anne used fake names, or pseudonyms, for the family in case she published her diary someday. She called them the van Daans.

Life in the annex was hard. There was no bathtub and limited hot water. Anne remained cheerful about her situation when writing in her diary:

I don't think I'll ever feel at home in this house, but that doesn't mean I hate it. It's more like being on vacation. . . . The Annex is an ideal place to hide in. It may be damp and lopsided, but there's probably not a more comfortable hiding place in all of Amsterdam. No, in all of Holland.

Peter van Pels's room in the Anne Frank House is set up to look as it did when he hid there.

FAMILIES SEPARATED

Many Jewish children didn't go into hiding with their parents. Their parents thought they'd have a better chance if they were sent to live with Christian families, in **convents**, or to orphanages. Some children had their hair dyed in an attempt to make them look less Jewish. Many were given new names as well. Many of these children survived, but never found their parents or families after the war.

FRITZ *Pfeffer*

In November 1942,
the Franks were joined by
Fritz Pfeffer. Anne called
him Alfred Dussel. He was
a dentist and shared a room
with Anne. She wrote: *"I'm
not exactly delighted at having
a stranger use my things, but
you have to make sacrifices for
a good cause."*

In November 1942,
the Franks were joined by
Fritz Pfeffer. Anne called
him Alfred Dussel. He was
a dentist and shared a room
with Anne. She wrote: *"I'm
not exactly delighted at having
a stranger use my things, but
you have to make sacrifices for
a good cause."*

Anne began to notice
that Pfeffer kept a lot of food
to himself, storing bread,
cheese, and other foods away
from the rest of the group.
She grew angry with him:
*"It's absolutely disgraceful that
Dussel, whom we've treated with
such kindness and whom we took
in to save from destruction, should
stuff himself behind our backs and not give us anything.
After all, we've shared all we had with him!"*

ANNE'S MATURITY

Anne's diary shows
that she was very
aware of how lucky
her family was: *"We're
so fortunate here, away
from the turmoil. We
wouldn't have to give a
moment's thought to all
this suffering if it weren't
for the fact that we're so
worried about those we
hold dear, whom we can
no longer help. . . . I get
frightened myself when I
think of close friends who
are now at the mercy of
the cruelest monsters ever
to stalk the earth. And all
because they're Jews."*

Like many young people, Anne Frank decorated her bedroom with pictures and photos.

LIFE *Continues in Secret*

Anne struggled with the relationships in her small world and turned to her diary for comfort: *"It's not easy trying to behave like a model child with people you can't stand, especially when you don't mean a word of it."*

She wasn't the only one who felt restless and on edge:

> **MORE TO KNOW**
>
> Anne made up pseudonyms for herself and her family, too. She was Anne Robin; Margot was Betty Robin; Otto was Frederik Robin; and Edith was Nora Robin.

Relationships here in the Annex are getting worse all the time. We don't dare open our mouths at mealtime (except to slip in a bite of food), because no matter what we say, someone is bound to resent it or take it the wrong way. . . . Sometimes I'm afraid my face is going to sag with all this sorrow and that my mouth is going to permanently droop at the corners. The others aren't doing any better."

This is the attic of the annex, where Anne would go when she wanted some quiet time.

"A PATCH OF BLUE"

Anne wrote a lot about the danger she felt: *"I see the eight of us in the Annex as if we were a patch of blue sky surrounded by menacing black clouds. The perfectly round spot on which we're standing is still safe, but the clouds are moving in on us, and the ring between us and the approaching danger is being pulled tighter and tighter. We're surrounded by darkness and danger . . ."*

The ARREST

On July 21, 1944, Anne wrote, *"Now I'm getting really hopeful, now things are going well at last. . . . Super news! An attempt has been made on Hitler's life."* However, on August 4, 1944, several Nazi policemen forced their way into the secret annex and arrested the Franks and the others. The Franks were questioned, jailed, and sent to the Westerbork camp in the northeastern Netherlands.

The Franks were placed in the punishment **barracks** for Jews who had gone into hiding. Anne, her sister, and her mother were put to work. Anne remained cheerful—she enjoyed being outside again. But on September 2, 1944, the eight people from the secret annex were sent by train to Auschwitz (OWSH-vihtz), a **concentration camp** in Poland.

LEFT BEHIND

The people who had been helping the Franks by bringing food and carrying messages faced trouble after the arrest as well. Johannes Kleiman and Victor Kugler were arrested and jailed. Jan and Miep Gies and Bep Voskuijl were questioned, but not arrested. It's believed that someone told the German secret police, called the Gestapo, about the secret annex, but no one knows who betrayed the Frank family. Miep and Bep found Anne's diary among the belongings left behind.

MORE TO KNOW

Anne began rewriting her diary because she wanted it published. The last diary entry Anne rewrote was March 29, 1944. Her last entry was August 1, 1944.

The staircase that led to the secret annex was hidden by a bookcase.

AUSCHWITZ
and Bergen-Belsen

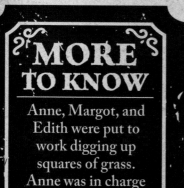

MORE TO KNOW

Anne, Margot, and Edith were put to work digging up squares of grass. Anne was in charge of giving out bread in the barracks.

The train to Auschwitz was so crowded there was no room to lie down during the 3-day trip. More than 1,000 prisoners were on the train. Upon arrival, they were examined by doctors. Because they were sick, over half of the prisoners were killed in the gas chambers. The other prisoners' heads were shaved and numbers were **tattooed** on their arms. There was little to eat and only dirty water to drink.

Those who knew Anne there said she maintained her cheerfulness when she could. Back in the annex, she had written: *"I am young and strong and am living a great adventure; I am still in the midst of it and can't grumble the whole day long. I have been given a lot, a happy nature, a great deal of cheerfulness and strength."*

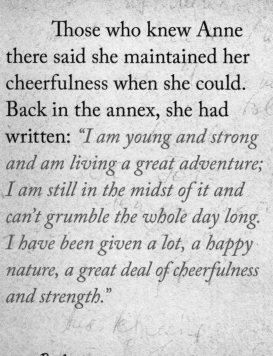

Birkenau was the largest of 39 camps that made up the Auschwitz complex. The majority of victims of Auschwitz died in Birkenau.

DEATH CAMP

Between 1940 and 1945, at least 960,000 Jews were killed in Auschwitz. The largest gas chamber could hold 2,000 people at one time. Prisoners were locked in this room and poisoned with deadly gas. Some prisoners were used in medical experiments. Others killed themselves by touching the electric fence that surrounded the camp. On January 27, 1945, the Soviet army entered Auschwitz and freed the remaining prisoners, most of whom were ill and dying.

Anne and Margot were transported to another concentration camp, Bergen-Belsen in Germany. There, Anne, Margot, and others slept in crowded tents at first. The Frank sisters' tent collapsed in a thunderstorm. Though they later moved into barracks, less and less food was given out as time went on.

Anne and Margot met people they had known from other camps and schoolmates from their life

HISTORY OF BERGEN-BELSEN

From 1940 to 1943, the Bergen-Belsen camp was a prisoner-of-war (POW) camp. As **Allied** forces marched into Germany in late 1944 and early 1945, Bergen-Belsen was used as a camp for thousands of Jewish prisoners moved from other sites. In July 1944, there were around 7,300 prisoners at Bergen-Belsen. The camp population rose to over 60,000 by April 1945. The crowded conditions meant days without food and quickly spreading diseases.

This is a view of the barracks of the Bergen-Belsen concentration camp in Germany in 1944.

in Amsterdam, which now seemed so far away. Talking with them was their only comfort. They worried about their parents.

Their mother Edith died from starvation at Auschwitz on January 6, 1945. She was found hiding bread that she was saving for the rest of her family. Both Frank sisters grew weak by early 1945. Margot became sick with **typhus**.

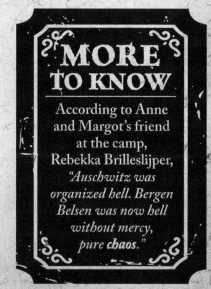

MORE TO KNOW

According to Anne and Margot's friend at the camp, Rebekka Brilleslijper, *"Auschwitz was organized hell. Bergen Belsen was now hell without mercy, pure **chaos**."*

ANNE'S *Death*

In February 1945, Anne found out her friend Hanneli Goslar was in Bergen-Belsen, on the other side of a fence. The Goslar family was going to be exchanged for German prisoners of war. Hanneli later remembered, *"A German was in a watchtower at the top of the fence. He wouldn't have asked a lot. He just would have shot me. I wasn't allowed to come near the fence. Not only me, but Anna [Anne] too."* Though the two girls weren't allowed to speak or be near the fence, Hanneli threw food to Anne.

Anne grew weak and caught typhus. Margot died in March 1945. Anne died a few days later. They were buried in an unknown mass grave. The prisoners at Bergen-Belsen were freed by the Allies just weeks later in April 1945.

WHO'S RESPONSIBLE?

In her diary, Anne wrote about the war. She didn't think it was only Hitler's fault: *"I don't believe that the big men . . . alone, are guilty of the war. Oh no, the little man is just as guilty, otherwise the peoples of the world would have risen in revolt long ago! There's in people simply an urge to destroy, an urge to kill."* She believed everyone has a responsibility to stand up to evil.

Although this gravestone was placed in Bergen-Belsen after the Frank sisters' deaths, it doesn't mark the exact location of their grave.

27

ANNE'S
Message Lives On

THE ANNE FRANK HOUSE

In the 1950s, the building that housed the secret annex was scheduled to be torn down. By this time, Anne's diary was very popular. People raised money to save the place where she and her family had hid. It became the Anne Frank House, a museum where visitors can see where Anne lived and wrote. Otto also started the International Youth Centre to teach young people about the dangers of hate and **discrimination**.

Anne's father Otto survived the war. He learned from people at the concentration camps what had happened to his family. After he returned to Amsterdam, Miep Gies gave him Anne's diary. Otto wanted it to be published, which had been Anne's great wish. After several unsuccessful attempts, a publisher finally accepted the book.

Anne's diary was first published in the Netherlands in 1947. In 1950, it was translated into French and German. In 1952, it was published in English as *Anne Frank: The Diary of a Young Girl.*

Anne wrote: *"I hope one thing only, and that is that this hatred of the Jews will be a passing thing, . . . for this is unjust!"* Anne and her diary will forever be a reminder of what hatred had done and should never be allowed to ever do again.

Parents can only advise their children or point them in the right direction. Ultimately, people shape their own characters.

I still believe, in spite of everything, that people are truly good at heart.

Go outside and try to recapture the happiness within yourself; think of all the beauty in yourself and in everything around you and be happy.

But where there's hope, there's life.

A person who's happy will make others happy; a person who has courage and faith will never die in misery!

I want to be useful or give pleasure to the people around me yet who don't really know me. I want to go on living, even after my death!

I know that I'm a woman, a woman with inward strength and plenty of courage!

MORE TO KNOW

Anne's diary has been turned into plays as well as movies.

GLOSSARY

Allied: having to do with the Allies, a group of nations in World War II (including England and the United States) that opposed the Axis nations (including Germany and Japan)

annex: a building that has been added on to another building

barrack: a temporary housing situation

chancellor: the chief minister in some kinds of governments

chaos: complete lack of order

concentration camp: one of the prison camps used for holding and killing prisoners in Nazi Germany

convent: a place where nuns live

decree: an official law or order

discrimination: unfairly treating people unequally because of their race or beliefs

Gypsy: a member of a traveling people who originated in northern India and now live mostly in south and southwest Asia, Europe, and North America

Nazi: having to do with the German political party led by Hitler during World War II. Also, a member of the German army under the leadership of Adolf Hitler.

Slav: someone from eastern Europe or northwestern Asia who speaks one of the Slavonic languages

synagogue: a temple or a house of prayer for Jewish people

tattoo: to mark the skin with a permanent design

typhus: a disease that causes fever, headaches, rashes, and more. It's spread by ticks and fleas carried by rodents.

FOR MORE
Information

Books

Frank, Otto H., and Mirjam Pressler, eds. *Anne Frank: The Diary of a Young Girl*. New York, NY: Alfred A. Knopf, 2010.

Hollingsworth, Tamara. *Anne Frank: A Light in the Dark*. Huntington Beach, CA: Teacher Created Materials, 2013.

Jacobson, Sid, and Ernie Colón. *Anne Frank: The Anne Frank House Authorized Graphic Biography*. New York, NY: Hill and Wang, 2010.

Websites

Anne Frank
www.annefrank.org/en/
Visit this website to find more information about Anne Frank, the Holocaust, and World War II.

Anne Frank
www.jewishvirtuallibrary.org/jsource/biography/frank.html
See the only existing film footage of Anne Frank.

Anne Frank & Her Diary
teacher.scholastic.com/frank/diary.htm
Read a timeline about the life and times of Anne Frank.

INDEX